FOR ORGANS, PIANOS & ELECTRONIC KEYBOARDS

E•Z PLAY TODAY

89

SONGS FOR CHILDREN

This E-Z Play TODAY book was created "especially for children."
In this book of 30 songs, there are:

- story songs
- activity songs
- campfire songs

- songs sung at home
- songs learned in school
- just plain fun songs

All of the music is written in E-Z Play TODAY notation and arranged so you can play instantly!

The songs appear in the book in an "easy-learning" sequence.

So, after you read about the special notation on the next two pages, you can begin by learning the first song.

Maybe even Mom and Dad will join in on the fun!

Contents

HAL•LEONARD®
CORPORATION
7777 W. BLUEMOUND RD. P.O. BOX 13819 Milwaukee, WI 53213

T0057327

Playing Preview

THE MELODY (Right Hand)

The melody of a song appears as large lettered notes on a staff. The letter name corresponds to a key on the keyboard of an organ.

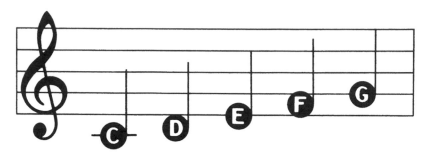

ACCOMPANIMENT (Left Hand)

The arrangements in this series have been written for all types of chord accompaniment.

1 One button (chord organ) or one-key chords.

2 Three-note (triad) chords.

3 Conventional, or standard chord positions.

Chord names, called chord symbols, appear above the melody line as either a boxed symbol ⬚C⬚

or as an alternate chord (**C7**)

or both **C7** / ⬚C⬚

1 For chord organ or one-key chords, play whichever chord name is on your unit.

2 If you are playing triad chords, follow the boxed symbols. A triad chord is played like this:

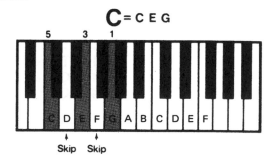

- Place your little finger on the key which has the same letter name as the chord.

- Skip a white key and place your middle finger on the next white key.

- Skip another white key and place your thumb on the next white key.

In some cases, there is an ARROW to the **left** or to the **right** of the chord name.

The arrow indicates moving one of the triad notes either to the **left** or to the **right** on the keyboard.

To understand this, first think of a chord symbol as having three sections, representing the three notes of the chord.

An ARROW is positioned next to the chord letter in one of these sections, indicating which of the three notes to change. For example:

• An arrow to the left means to move a note of the chord **down** (left) to the next adjacent key.

In this example where the arrow is in the **lower left**, or "1" position, move the first note "B" **down** to the black key B♭.

• An arrow to the right means to move a note of the chord **up** (right) to the next adjacent key.

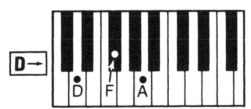

In this example where the arrow is in the **middle**, or "2" position, move the middle note **up** to the black key F♯.

3 If you are playing standard chord positions, play the chord in the boxed symbol, unless an alternate chord is indicated. Play alternate chords whenever possible.

For your reference, a Chord Speller Chart of standard chord positions appears in the back of this book.

REGISTRATION AND RHYTHM

A Registration number is shown above the music for each song. This number corresponds to the same number on the Registration Guide which appears on the inside front cover of this book. The Registration numbers also correspond to the numbers on the E-Z Play TODAY Registration Guides that are available for many brands of organs. See your organ dealer for the details.

You may wish to select your own favorite registration or perhaps experiment with different voice combinations. Then add an automatic rhythm...and HAVE FUN.

Mary Had A Little Lamb

Registration 4

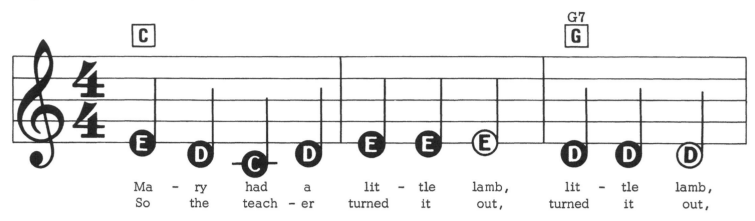

Ma - ry had a lit - tle lamb, lit - tle lamb,
So the teach - er turned it out, turned it out,

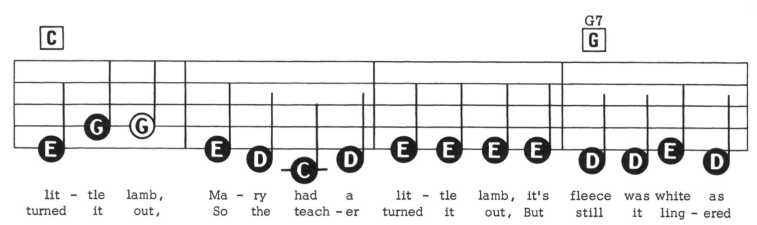

lit - tle lamb, Ma - ry had a lit - tle lamb, it's fleece was white as
turned it out, So the teach - er turned it out, But still it ling - ered

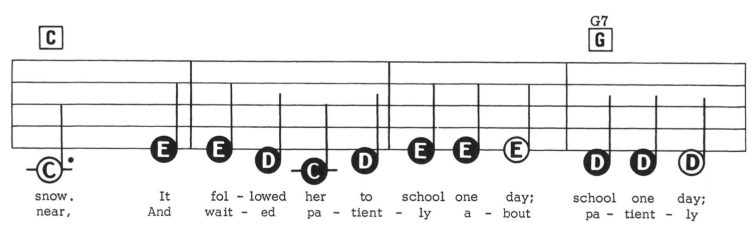

snow. It fol - lowed her to school one day; school one day;
near, And wait - ed pa - tient - ly a - bout pa - tient - ly

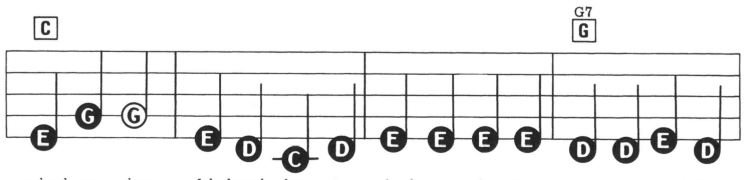

school one day; fol - lowed her to school one day; Which was a - gainst the
pa - tient - ly wait - ed pa - tient - ly a - bout Till Ma - ry did ap -

5
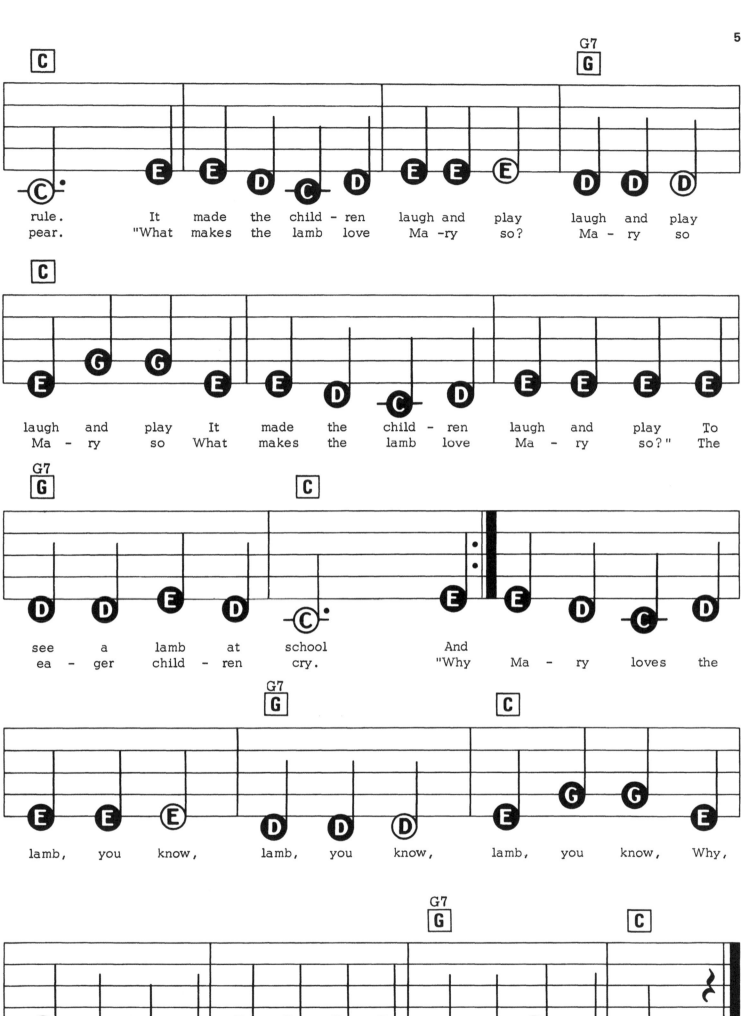
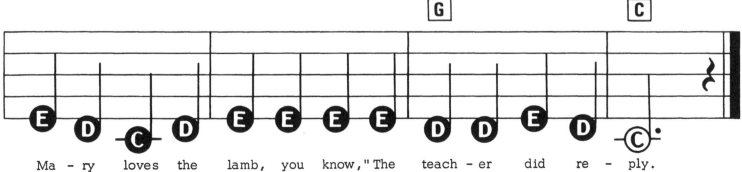

Baa, Baa Black Sheep

Registration 2

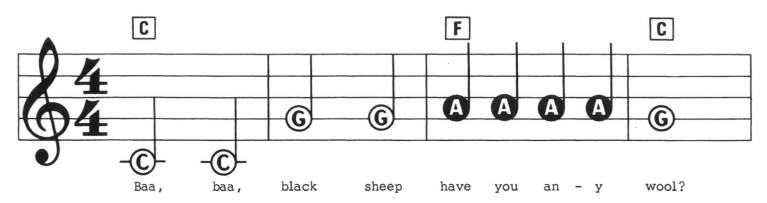

Baa, baa, black sheep have you an - y wool?

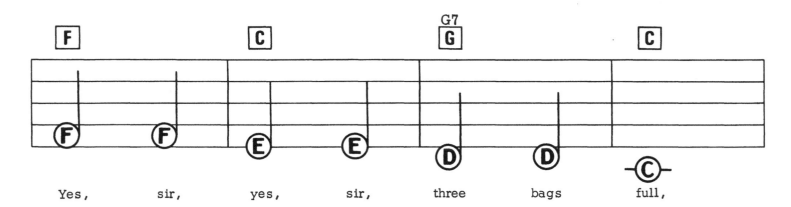

Yes, sir, yes, sir, three bags full,

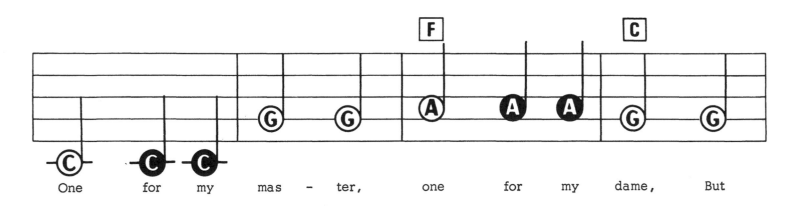

One for my mas - ter, one for my dame, But

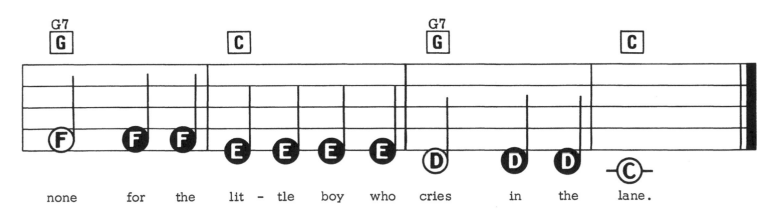

none for the lit - tle boy who cries in the lane.

Hickory Dickory Dock

Registration 1

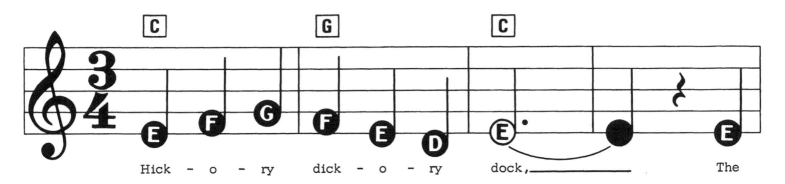

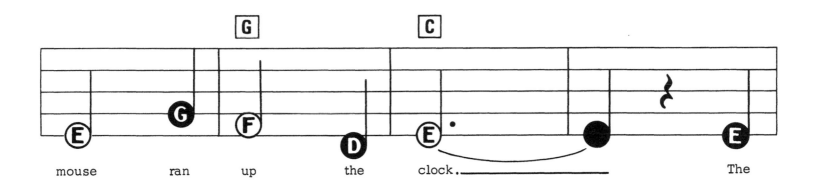

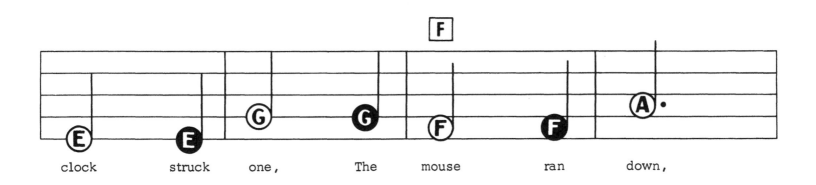

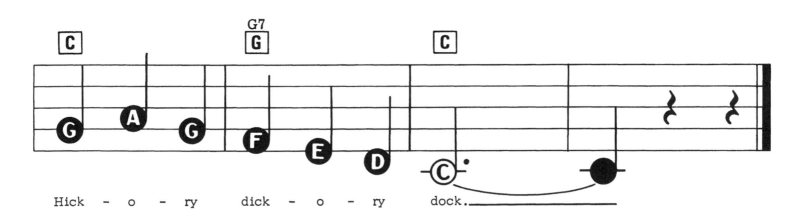

Hey, Diddle Diddle

Registration 3

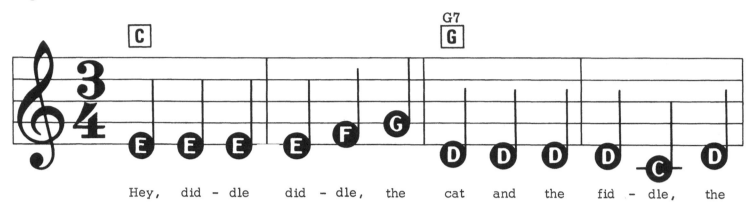

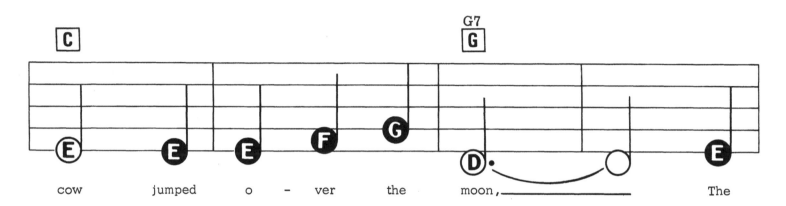

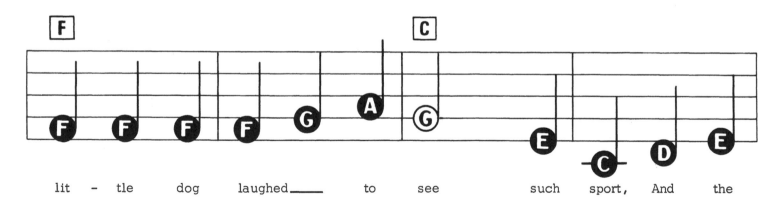

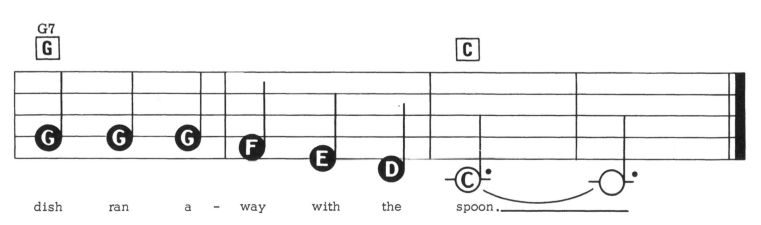

Hot Cross Buns

Registration 5

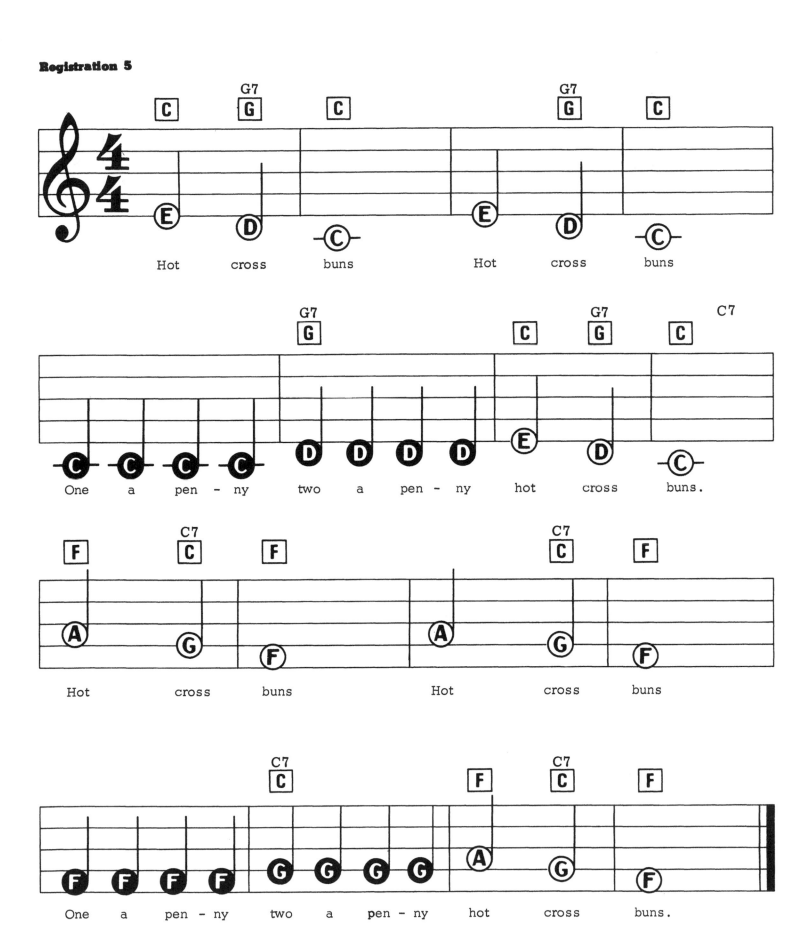

London Bridge

Registration 8

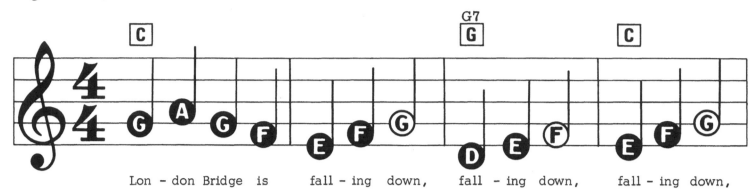

Lon - don Bridge is fall - ing down, fall - ing down, fall - ing down,

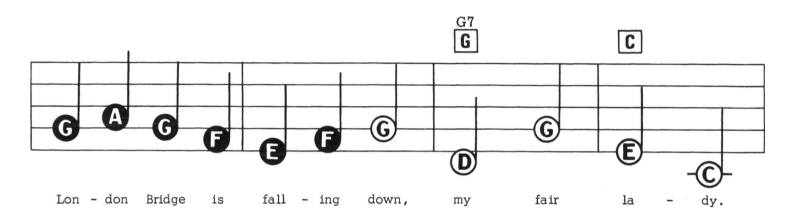

Lon - don Bridge is fall - ing down, my fair la - dy.

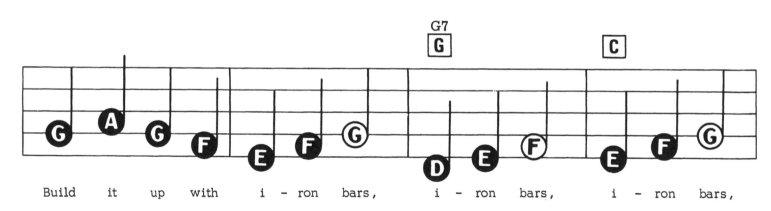

Build it up with i - ron bars, i - ron bars, i - ron bars,

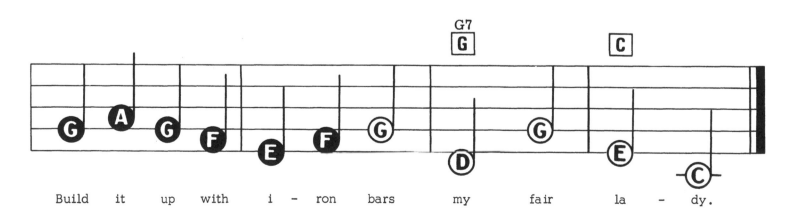

Build it up with i - ron bars my fair la - dy.

Blow The Man Down

Registration 9

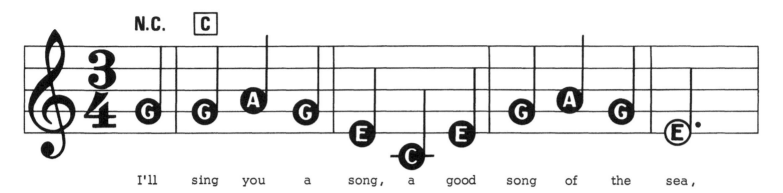

I'll sing you a song, a good song of the sea,

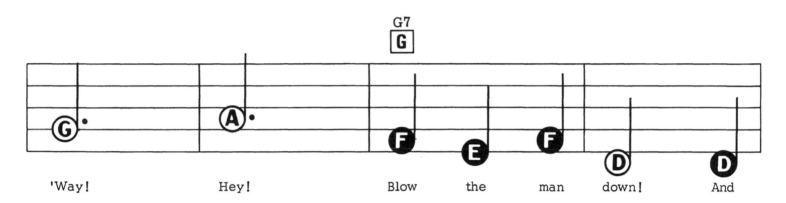

'Way! Hey! Blow the man down! And

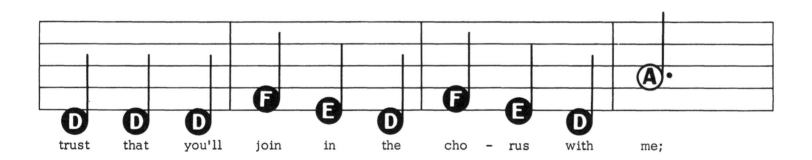

trust that you'll join in the cho - rus with me;

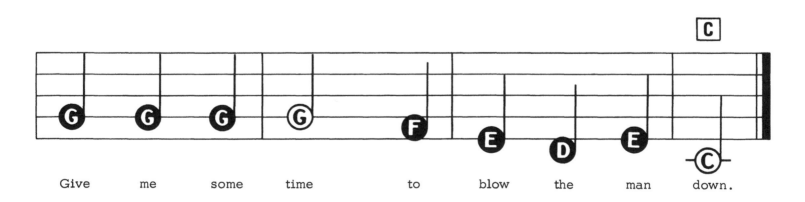

Give me some time to blow the man down.

Row, Row, Row Your Boat

Registration 5

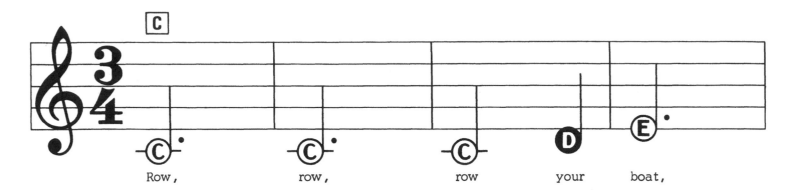

Row, row, row your boat,

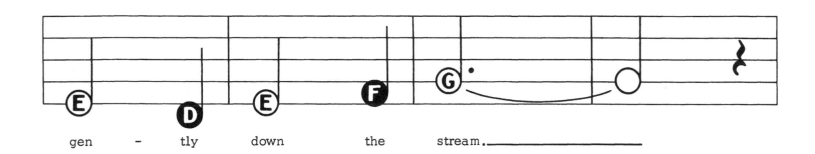

gen - tly down the stream.

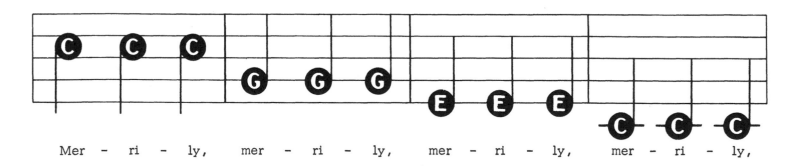

Mer - ri - ly, mer - ri - ly, mer - ri - ly, mer - ri - ly,

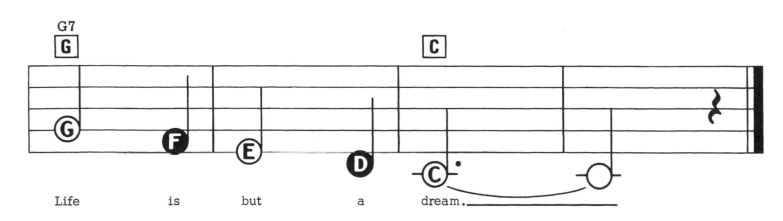

Life is but a dream.

The Farmer In The Dell

Registration 3

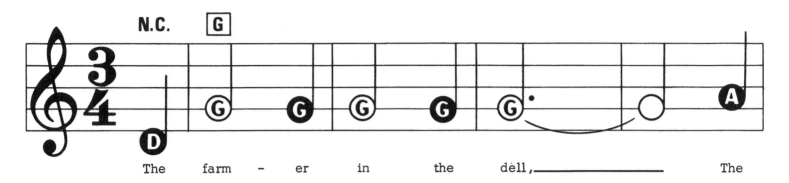

The farm – er in the dell, _____ The

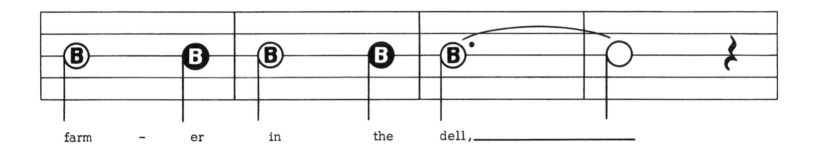

farm – er in the dell, _____

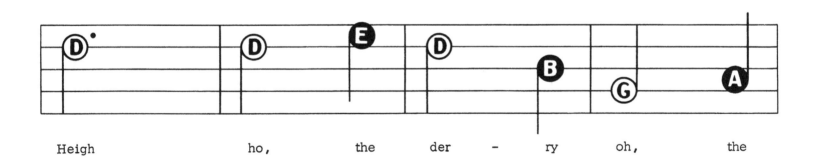

Heigh ho, the der – ry oh, the

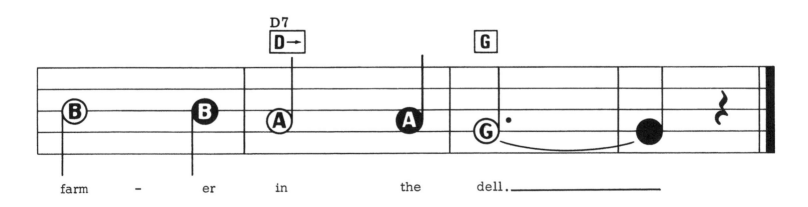

farm – er in the dell. _____

Three Blind Mice

Registration 1

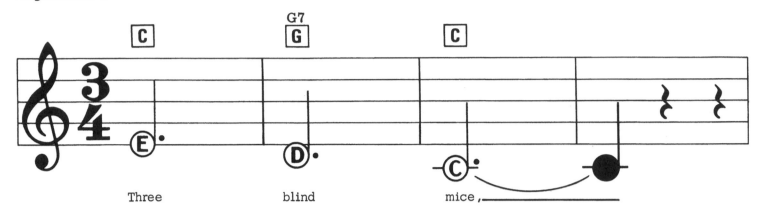

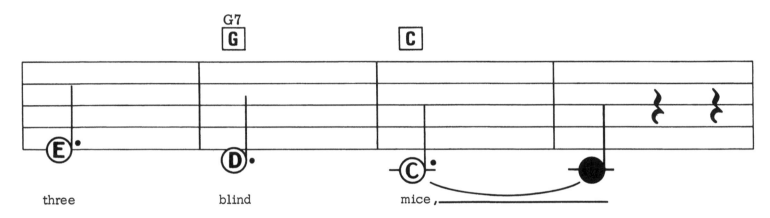

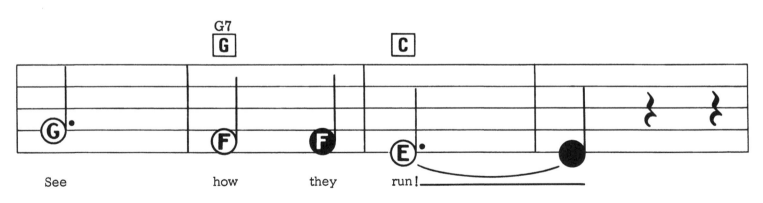

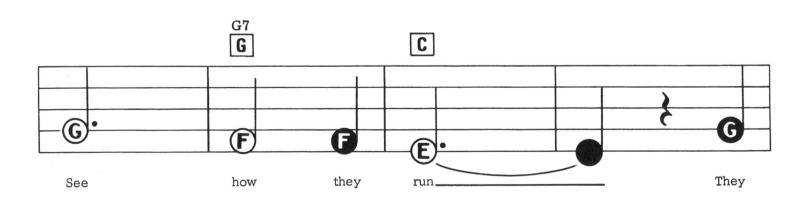

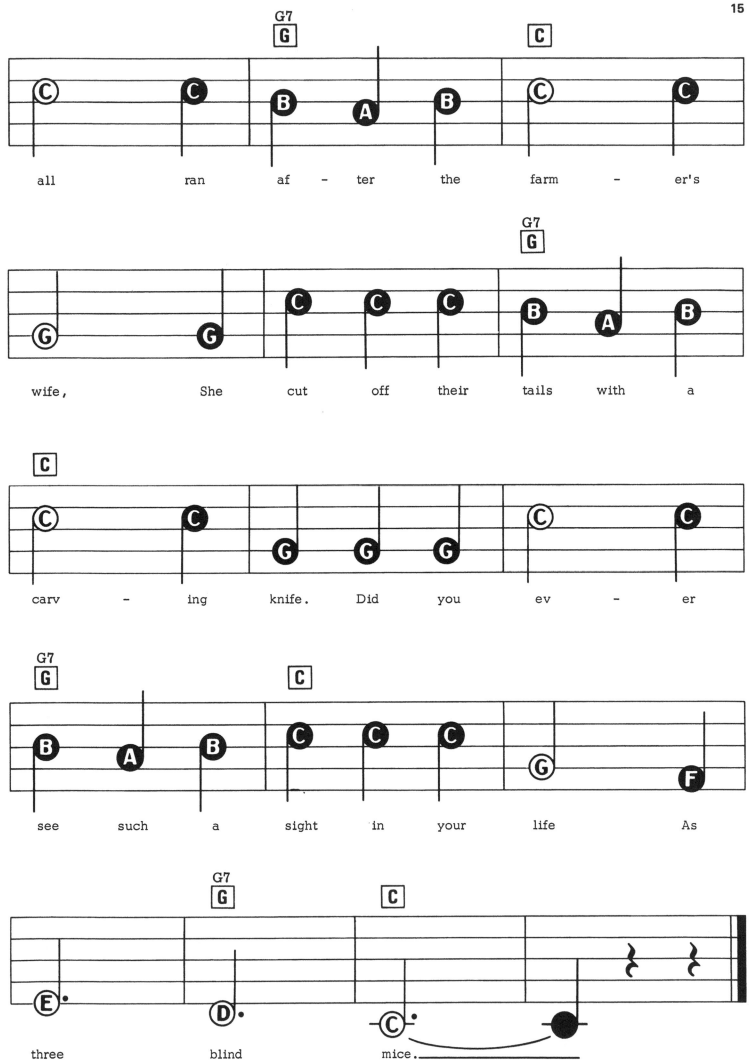

Mulberry Bush

Registration 5

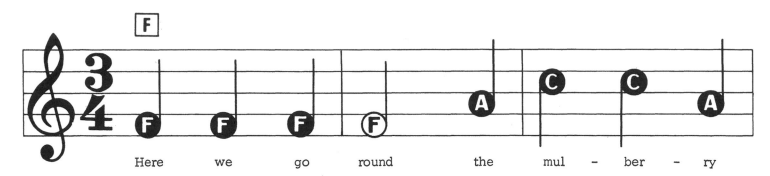

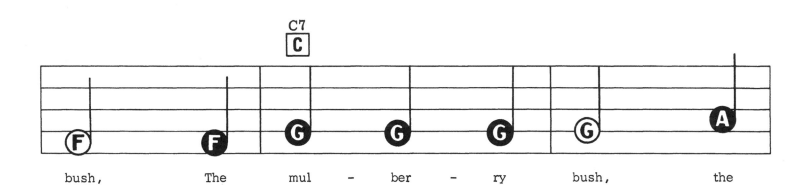

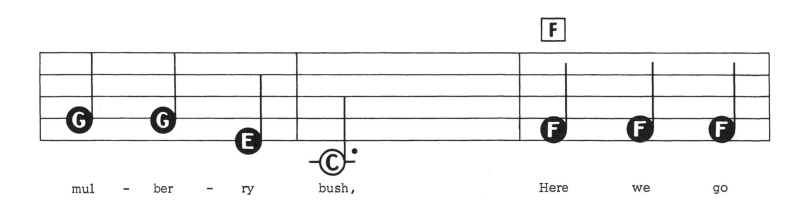

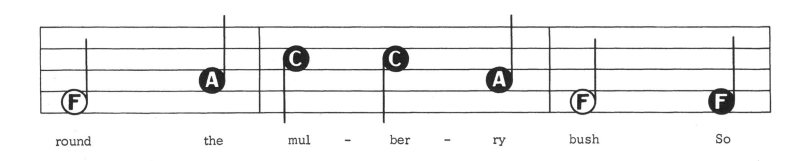

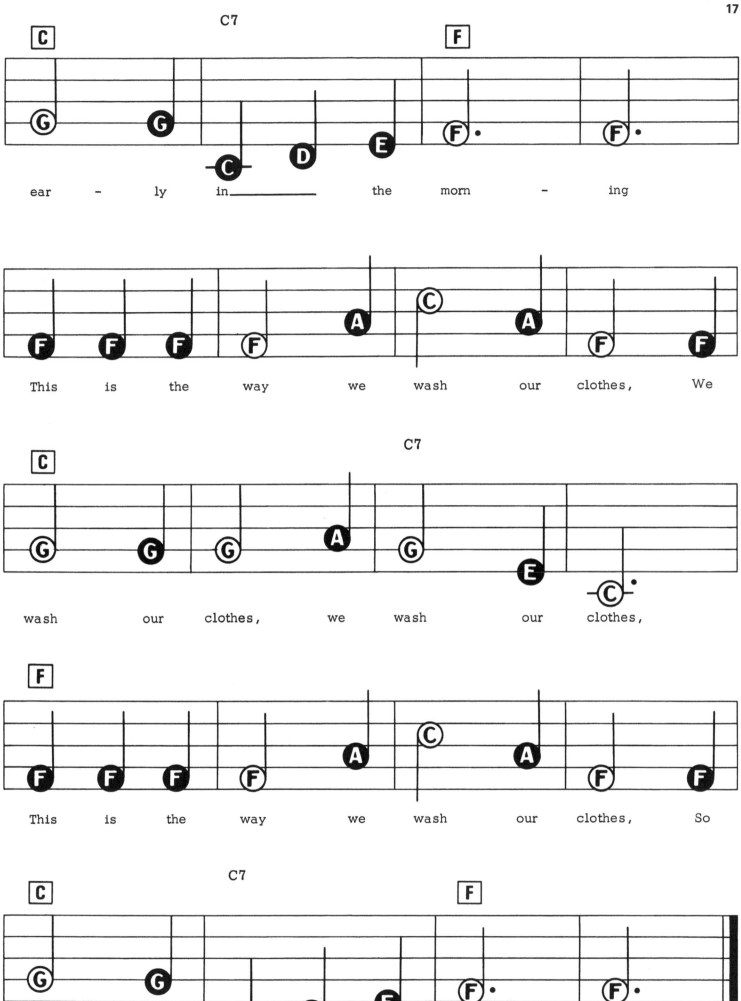

Little Bo-Peep

Registration 2

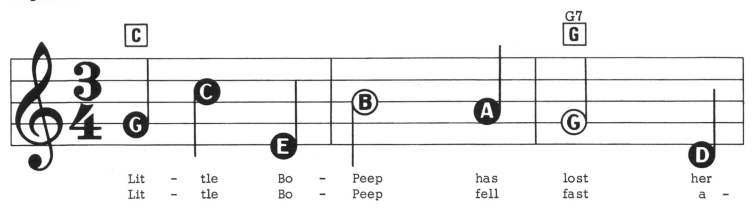

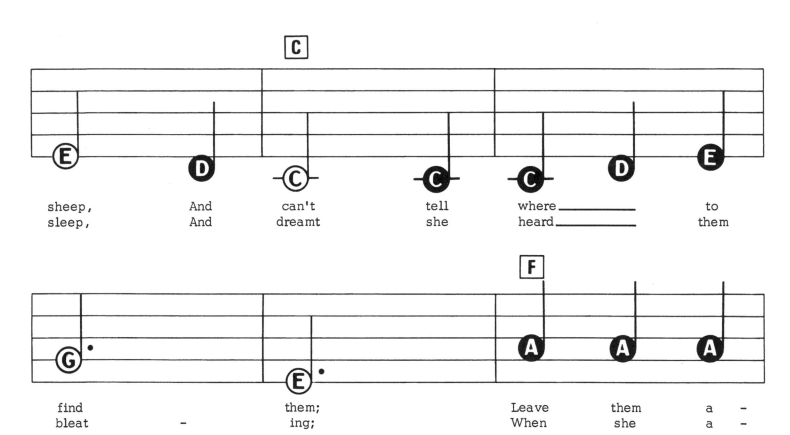

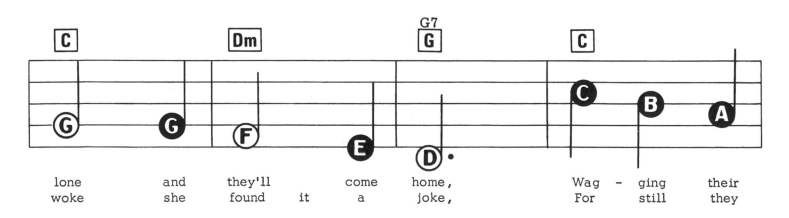

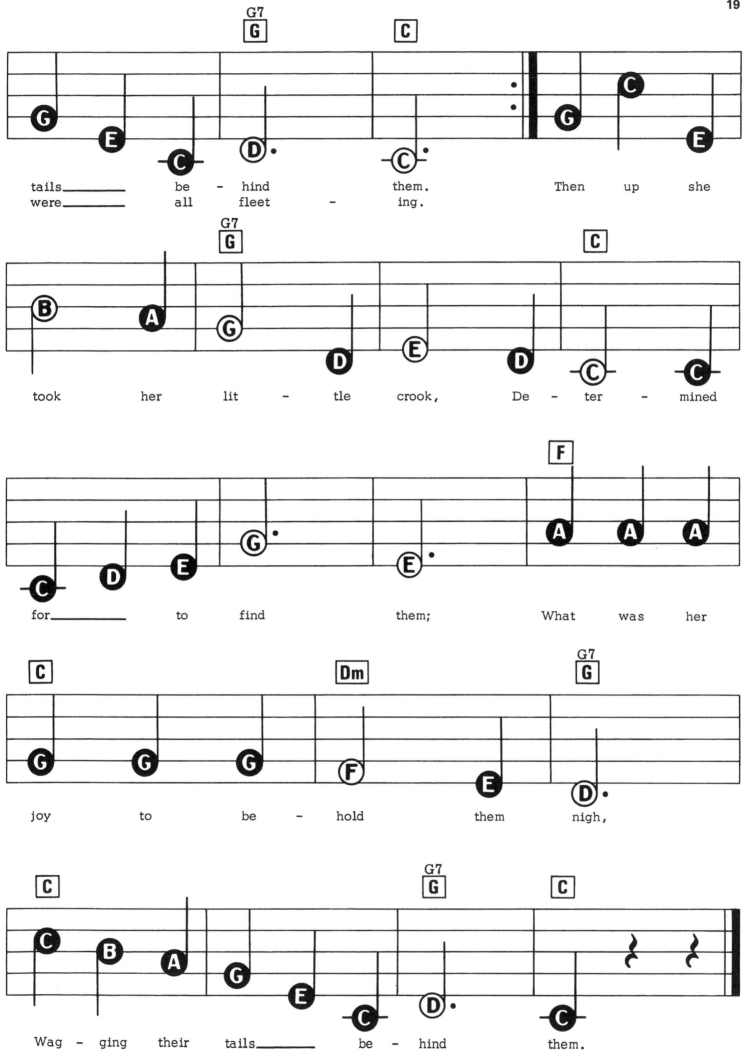

tails_____ be - hind them. Then up she
were_____ all fleet - ing.

took her lit - tle crook, De - ter - mined

for_____ to find them; What was her

joy to be - hold them nigh,

Wag - ging their tails_____ be - hind them.

Jack And Jill

Registration 4

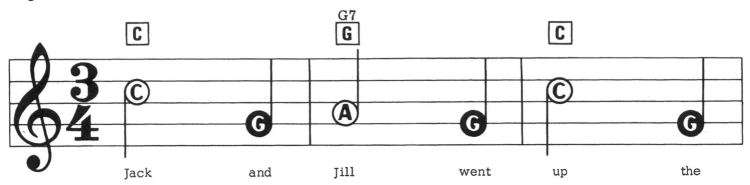

Jack and Jill went up the

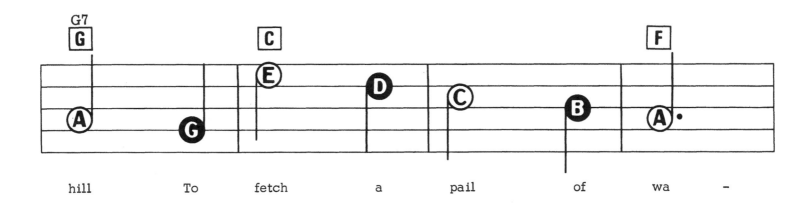

hill To fetch a pail of wa -

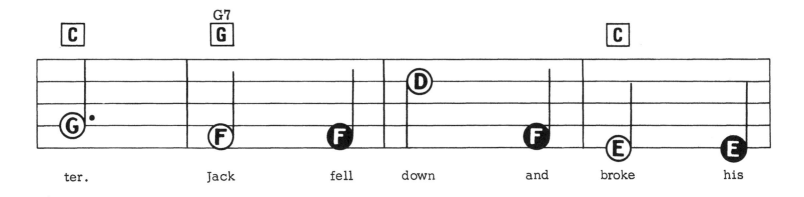

ter. Jack fell down and broke his

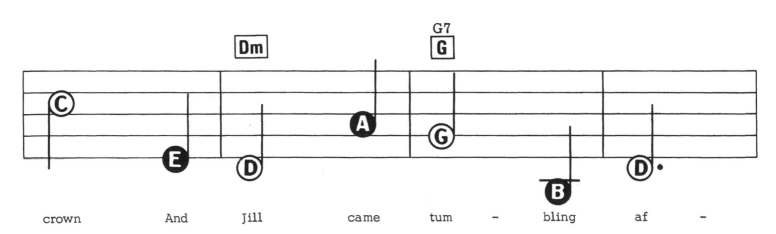

crown And Jill came tum - bling af -

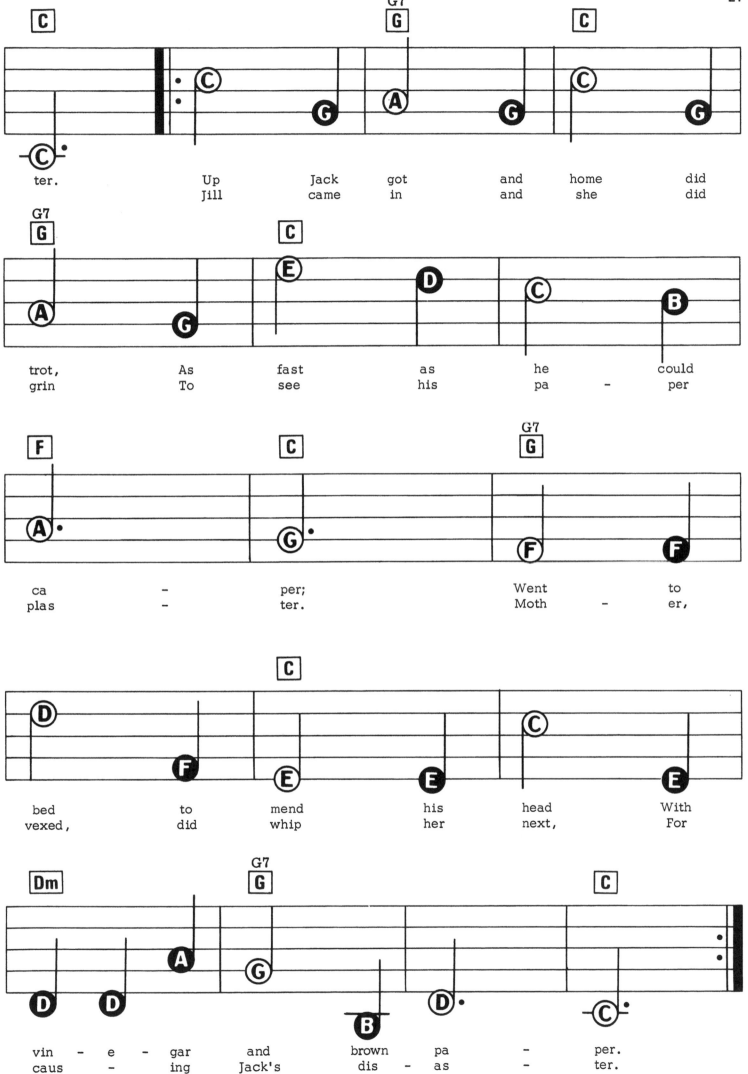

The Campbells Are Coming

Registration 3

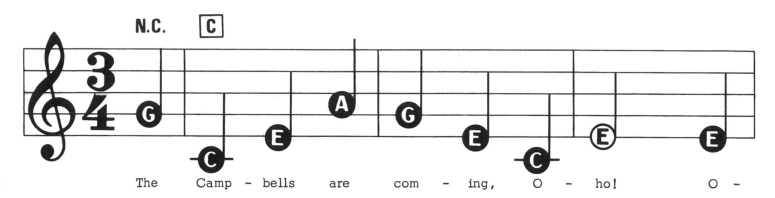

The Camp - bells are com - ing, O - ho! O -

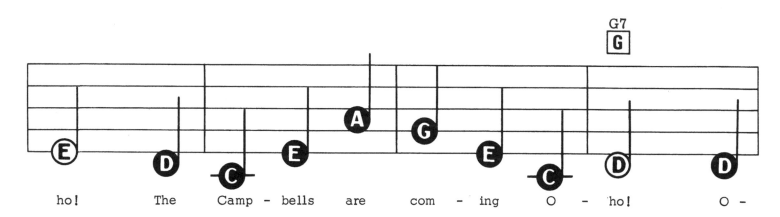

ho! The Camp - bells are com - ing O - ho! O -

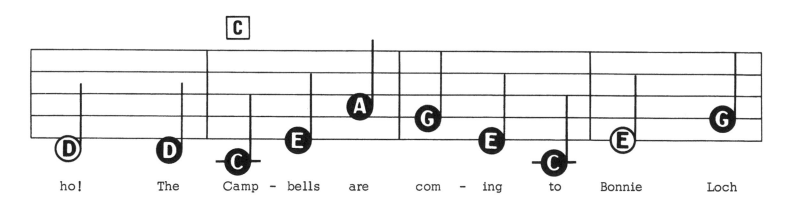

ho! The Camp - bells are com - ing to Bonnie Loch

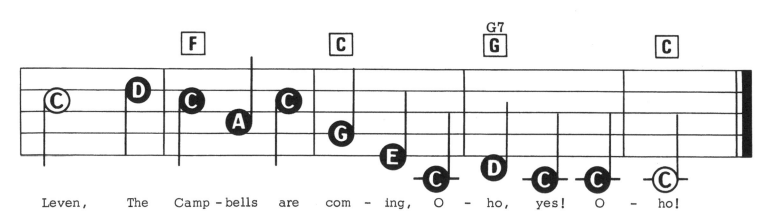

Leven, The Camp - bells are com - ing, O - ho, yes! O - ho!

Little Jack Horner

Registration 1

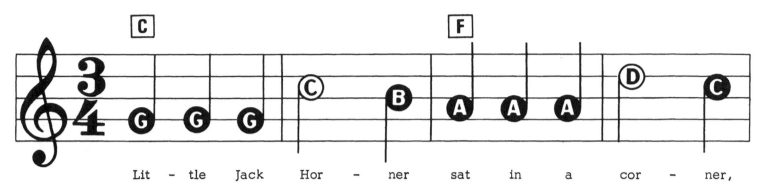

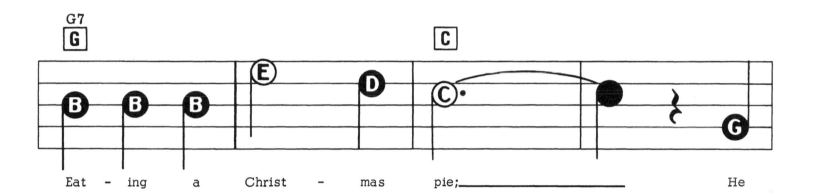

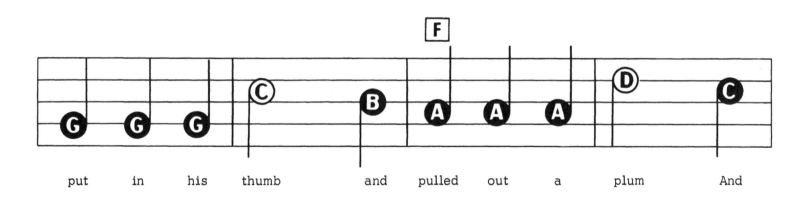

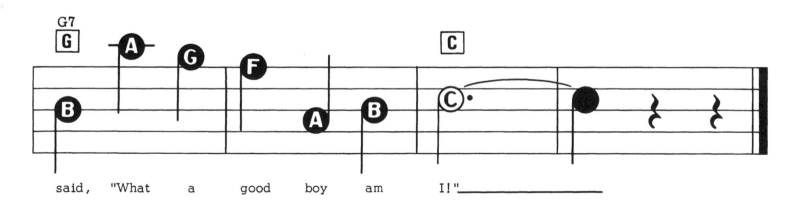

Sing A Song Of Sixpence

Registration 4

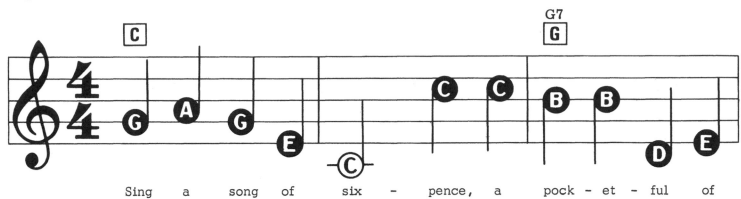

Sing a song of six - pence, a pock - et - ful of

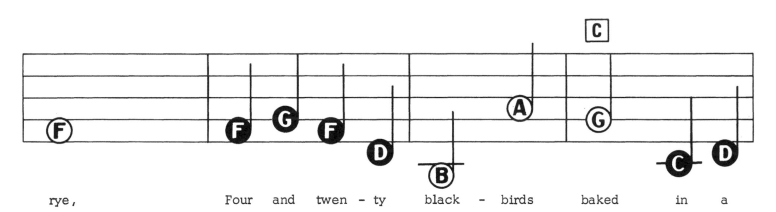

rye, Four and twen - ty black - birds baked in a

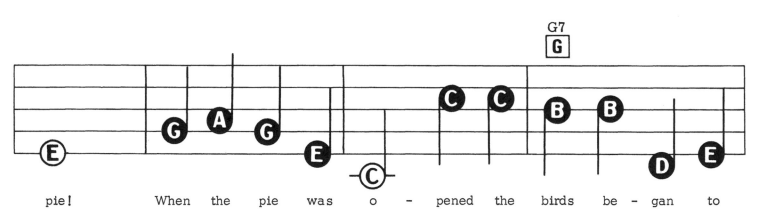

pie! When the pie was o - pened the birds be - gan to

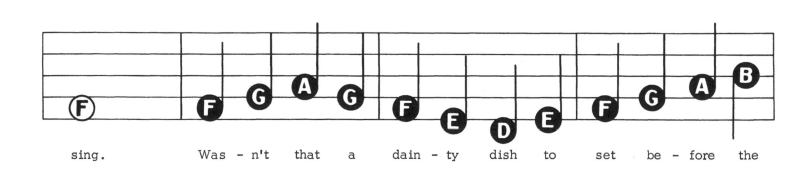

sing. Was - n't that a dain - ty dish to set be - fore the

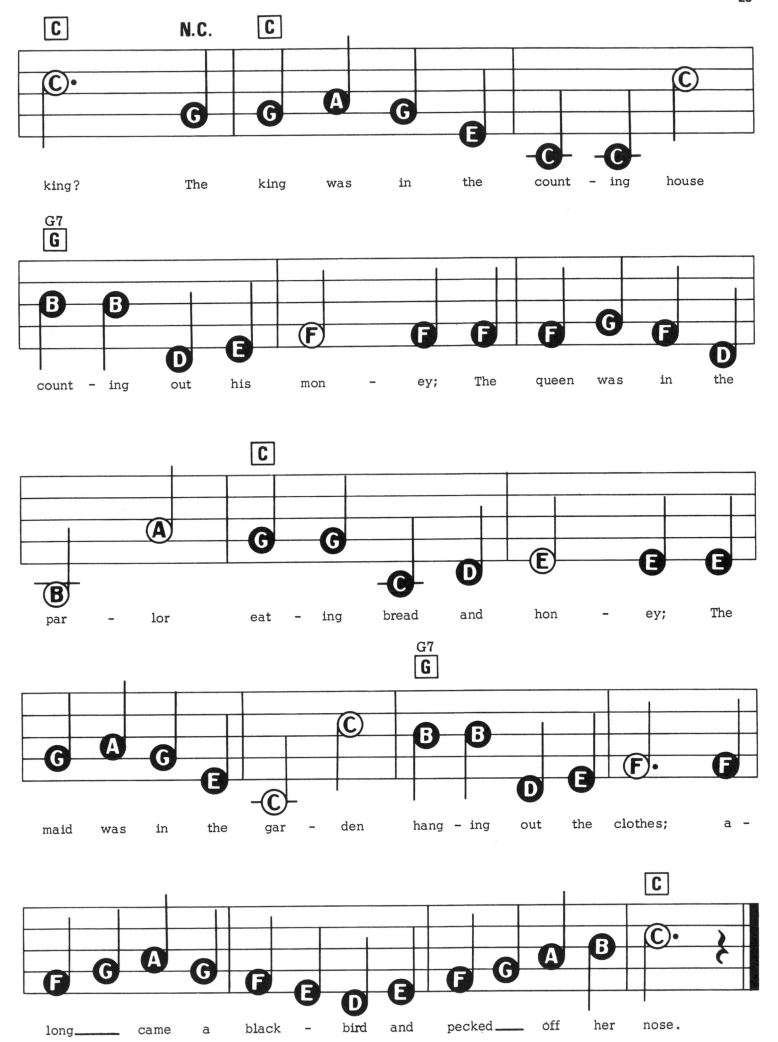

See Saw, Margery Daw

Registration 3

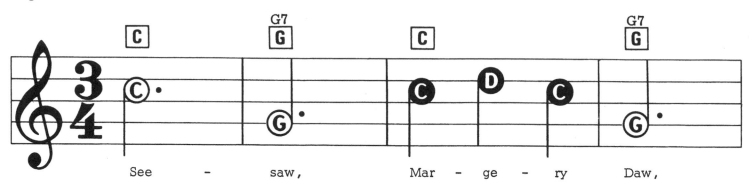

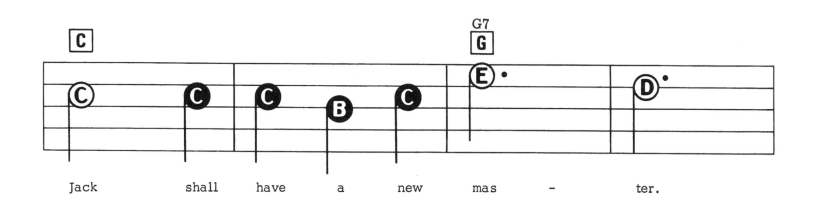

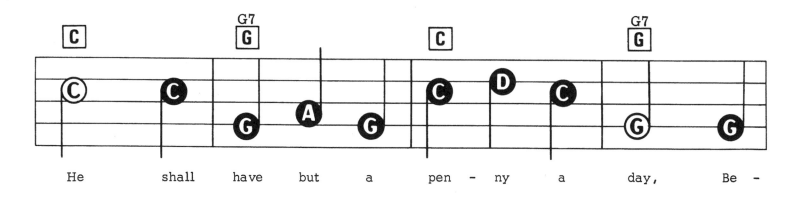

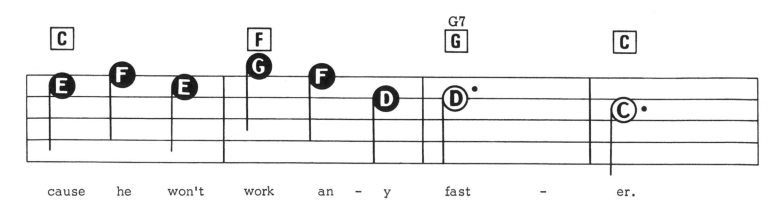

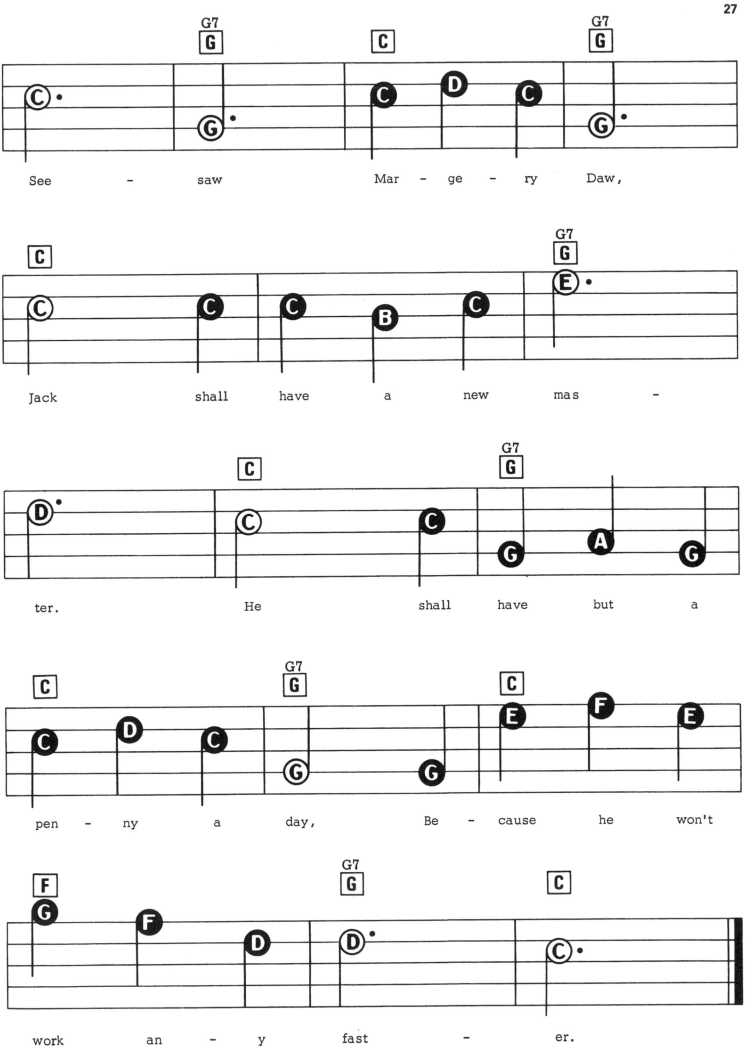

Looby Loo

Registration 2

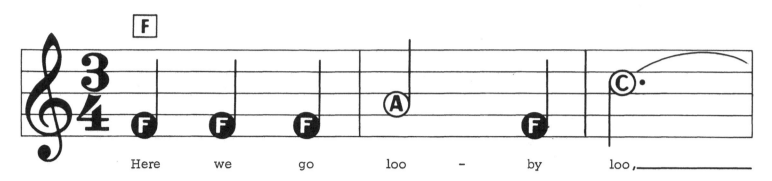

Here we go loo - by loo,

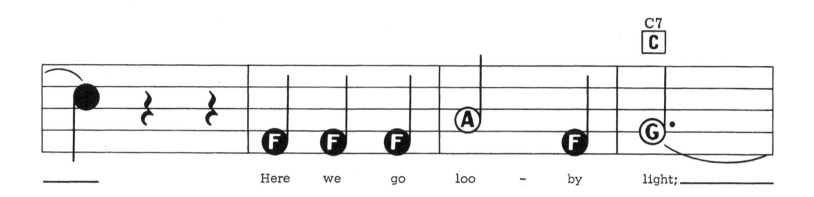

Here we go loo - by light;

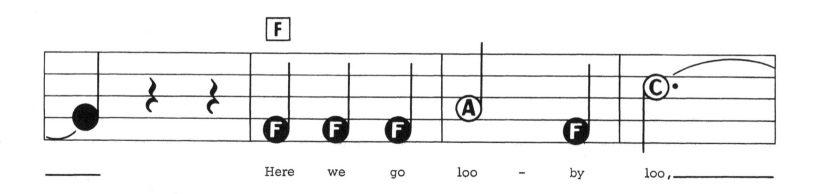

Here we go loo - by loo,

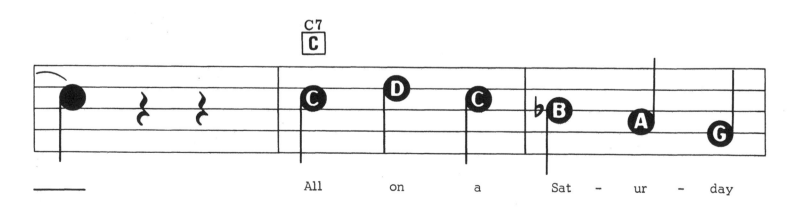

All on a Sat - ur - day

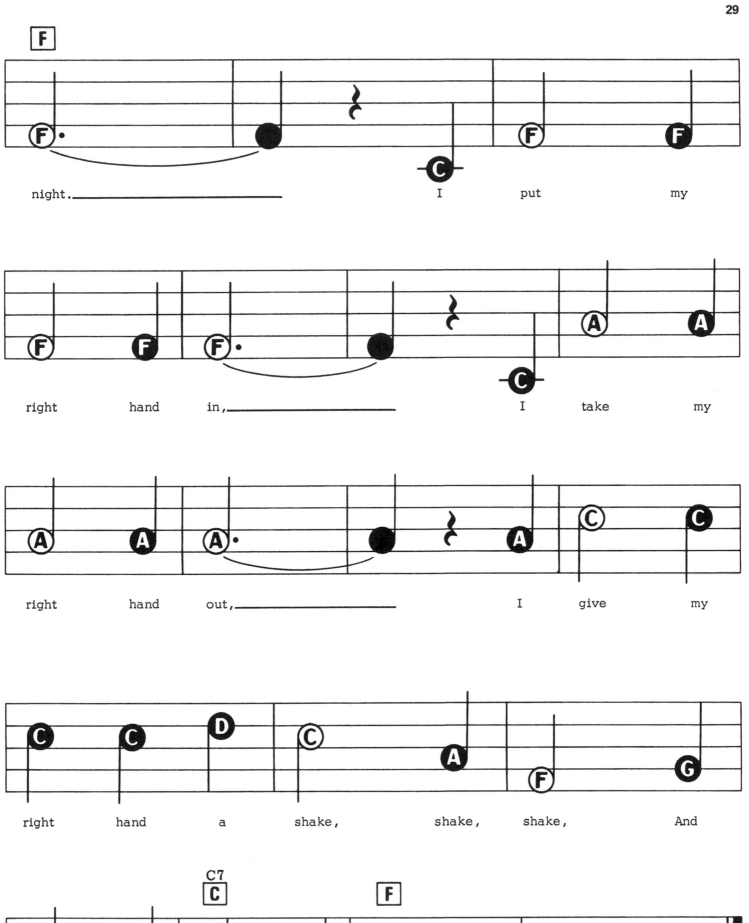

F
night. I put my
right hand in, I take my
right hand out, I give my
right hand a shake, shake, shake, And
C7
C
F
turn my - self a - bout.

Reuben And Rachel

Registration 5

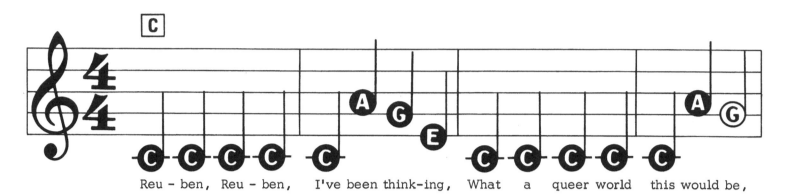

Reu - ben, Reu - ben, I've been think-ing, What a queer world this would be,

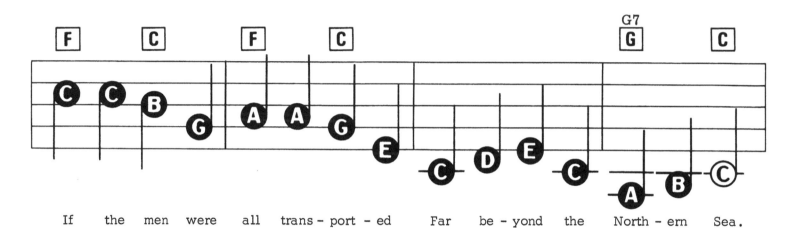

If the men were all trans - port - ed Far be - yond the North - ern Sea.

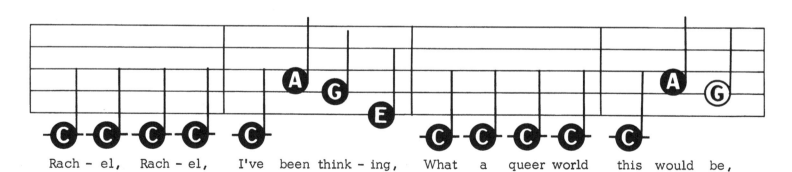

Rach - el, Rach - el, I've been think - ing, What a queer world this would be,

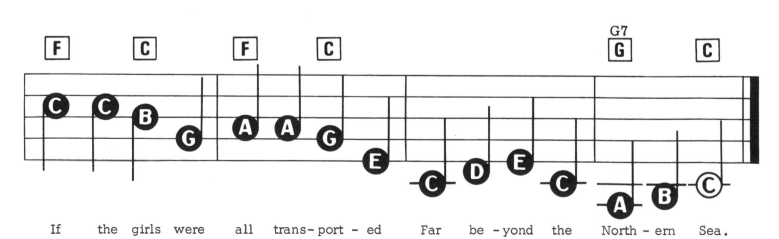

If the girls were all trans - port - ed Far be - yond the North - ern Sea.

Simple Simon

Registration 9

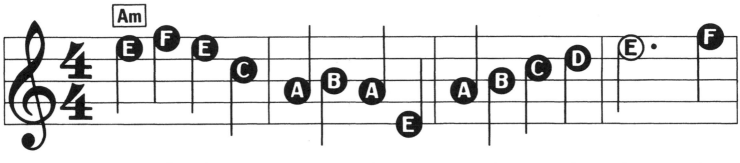

Sim - ple Si - mon met a pie - man go - ing to the fair, Says

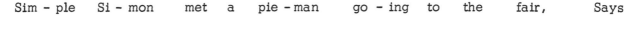

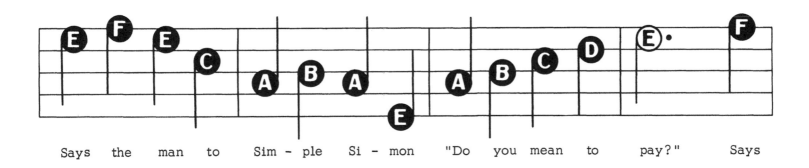

Sim - ple Si - mon to the pie - man "Let me taste your ware."

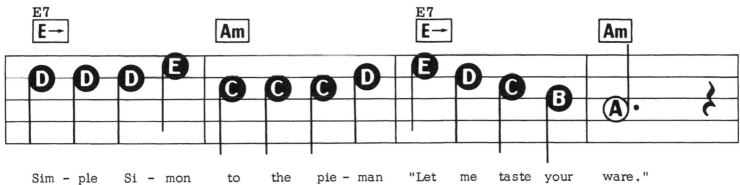

Says the man to Sim - ple Si - mon "Do you mean to pay?" Says

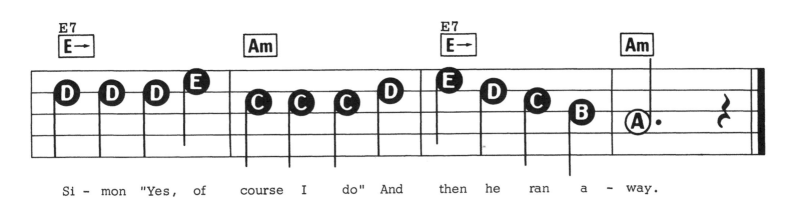

Si - mon "Yes, of course I do" And then he ran a - way.

Alphabet Song

Registration 8

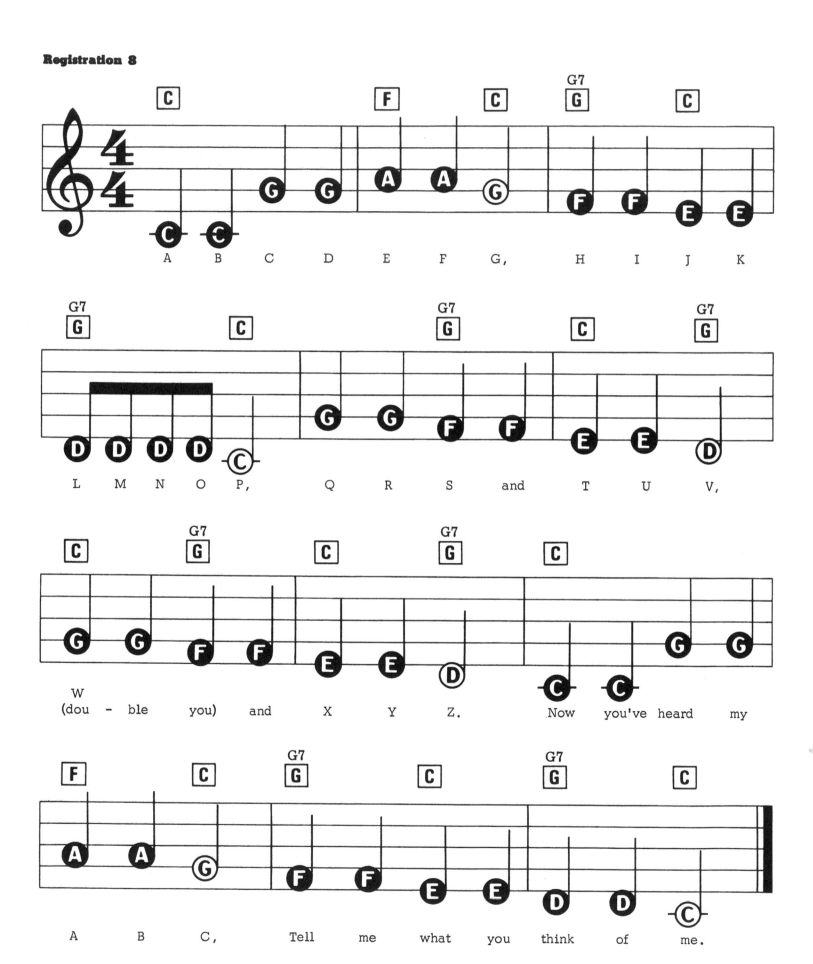

Polly, Put The Kettle On

Registration 4

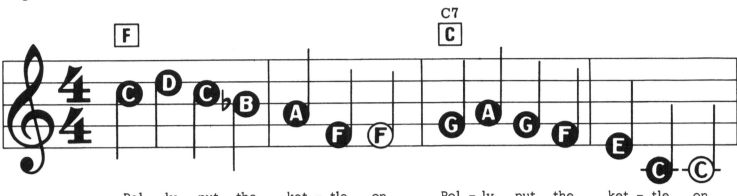

Pol - ly, put the ket - tle on, Pol - ly put the ket - tle on,

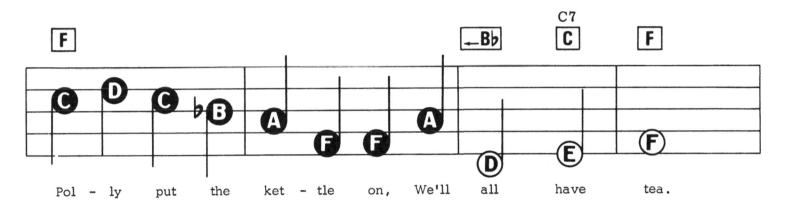

Pol - ly put the ket - tle on, We'll all have tea.

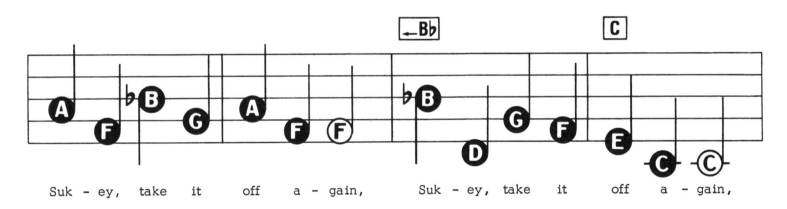

Suk - ey, take it off a - gain, Suk - ey, take it off a - gain,

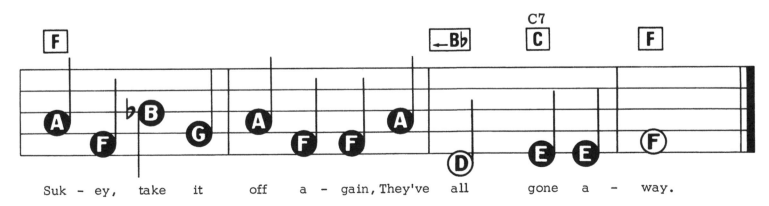

Suk - ey, take it off a - gain, They've all gone a - way.

Pat-A-Cake

Registration 4

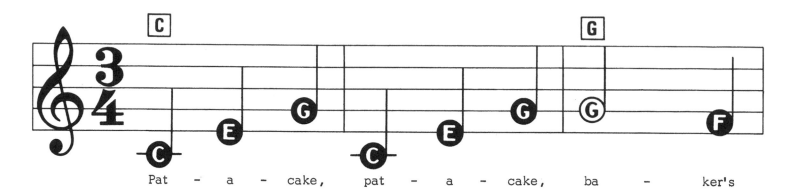

Pat - a - cake, pat - a - cake, ba - ker's

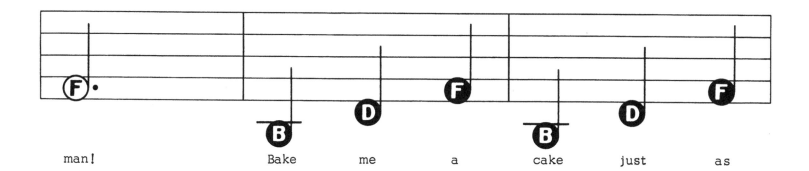

man!　　Bake　me　a　cake　just　as

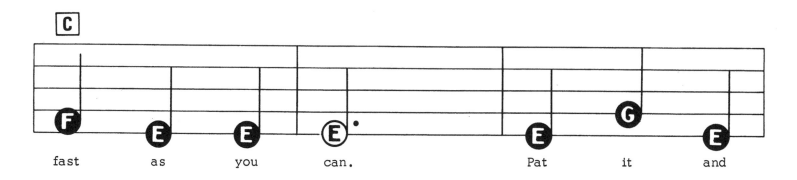

fast　as　you　can.　　Pat　it　and

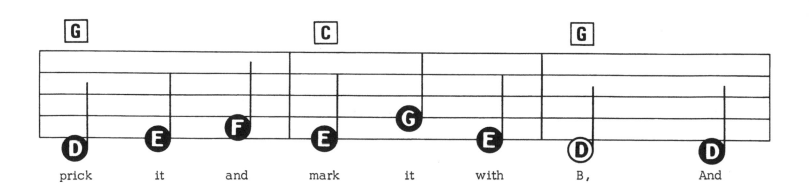

prick　it　and　mark　it　with　B,　And

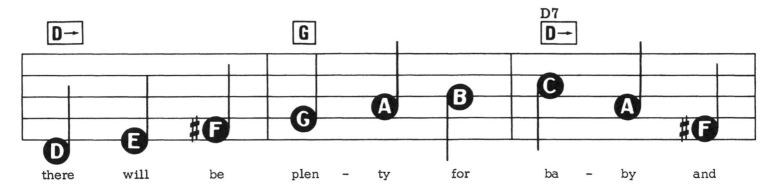

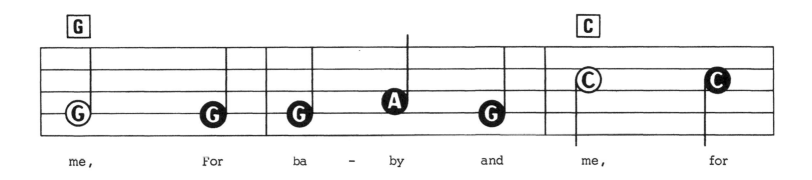

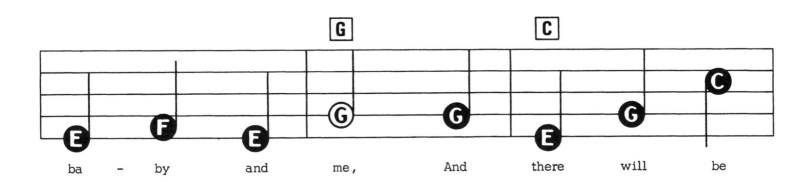

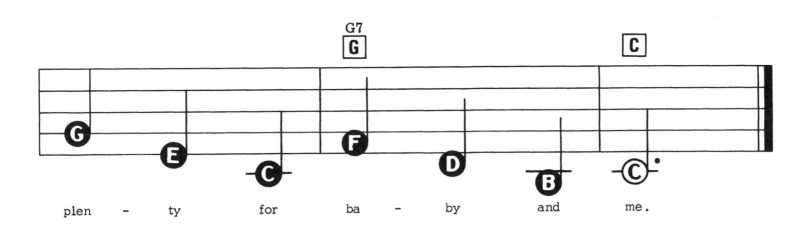

The Bear Went Over The Mountain

Registration 9

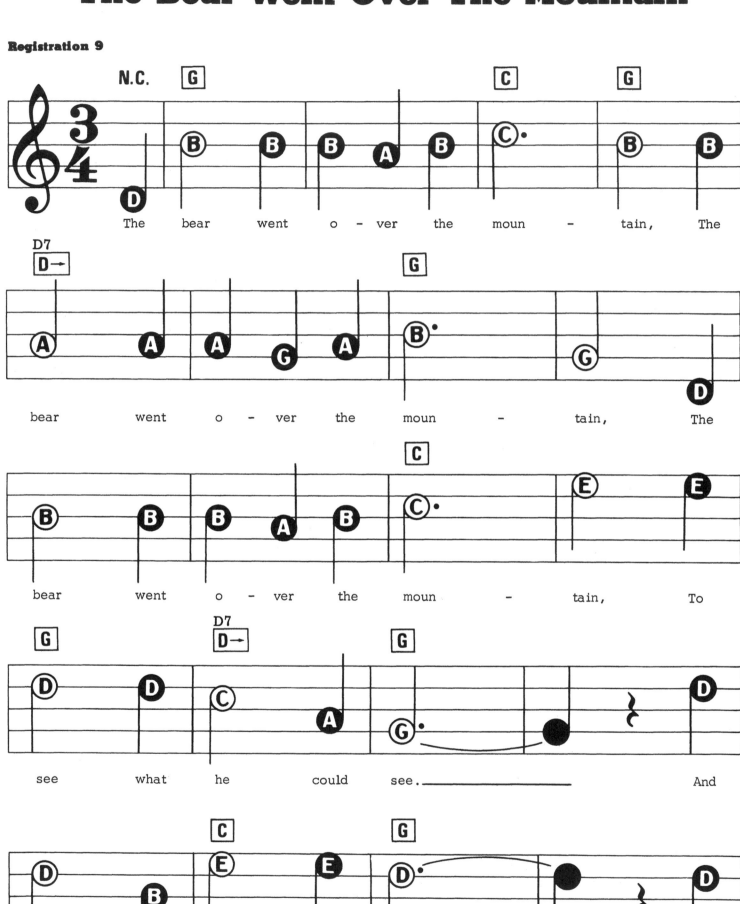

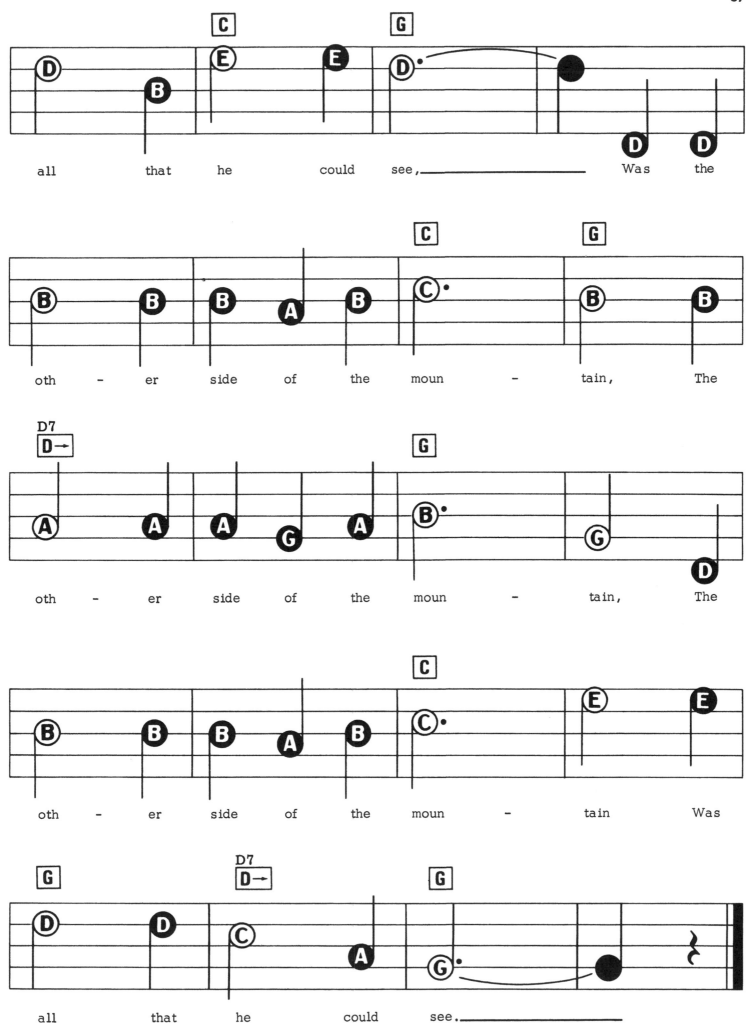

37

Sailor's Hornpipe

Registration 1

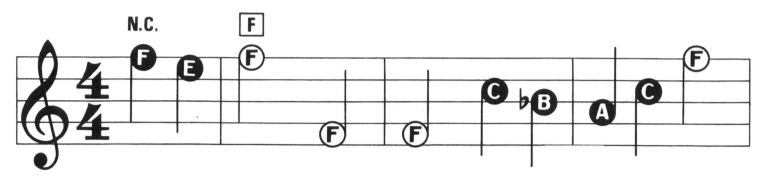

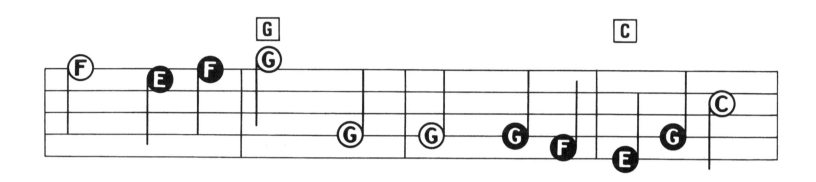

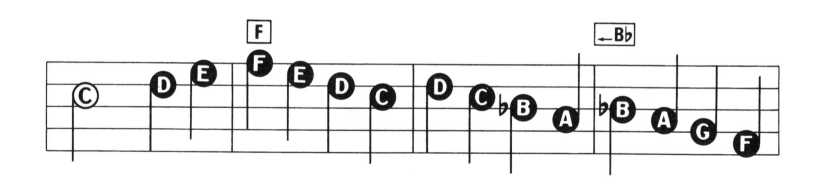

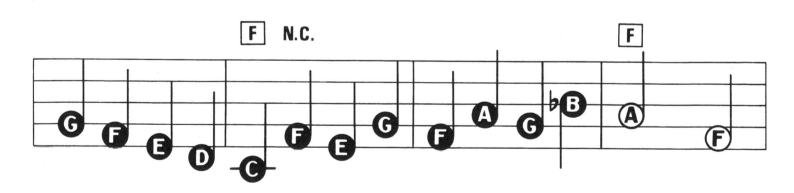

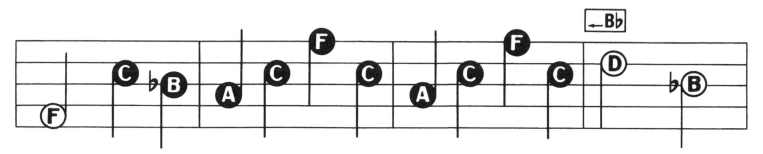

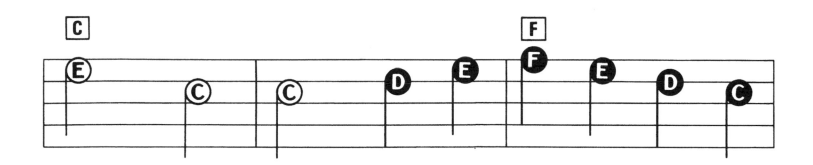

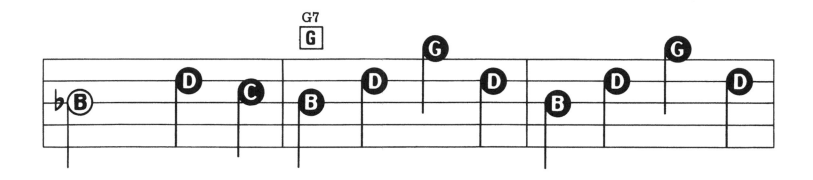

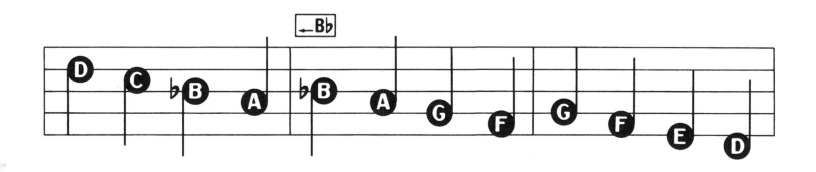

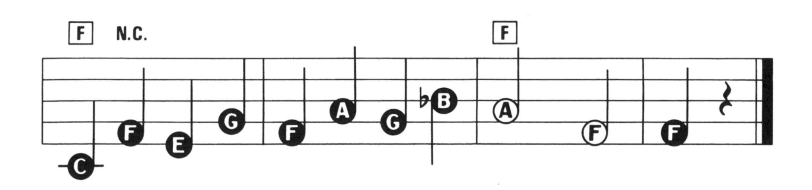

Are You Sleeping

Registration 4

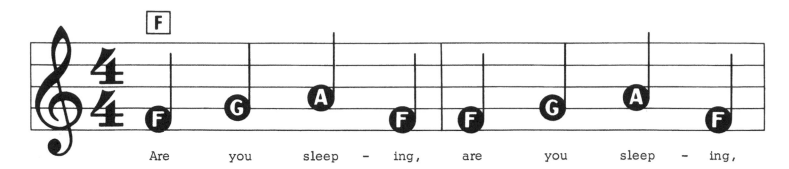

Are you sleep - ing, are you sleep - ing,

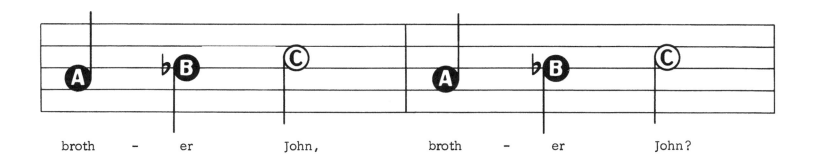

broth - er John, broth - er John?

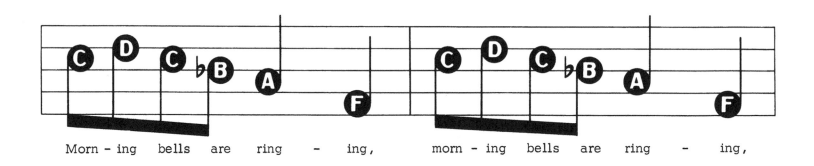

Morn - ing bells are ring - ing, morn - ing bells are ring - ing,

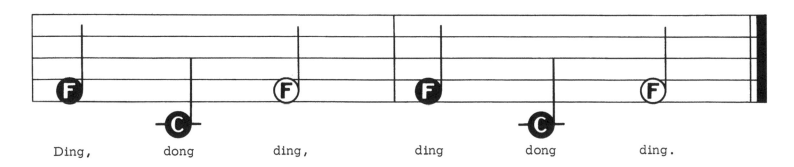

Ding, dong ding, ding dong ding.

Ten Little Indians

Registration 1

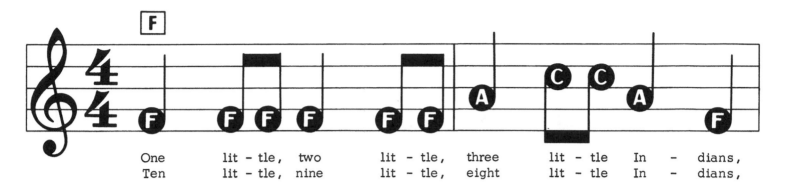

One lit - tle, two lit - tle, three lit - tle In - dians,
Ten lit - tle, nine lit - tle, eight lit - tle In - dians,

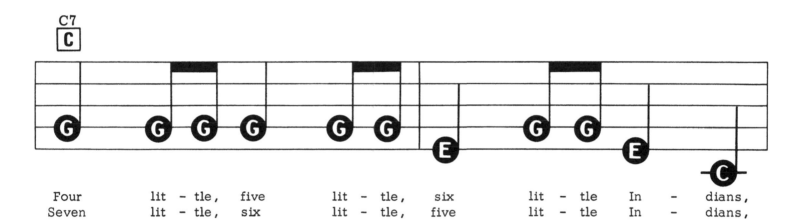

Four lit - tle, five lit - tle, six lit - tle In - dians,
Seven lit - tle, six lit - tle, five lit - tle In - dians,

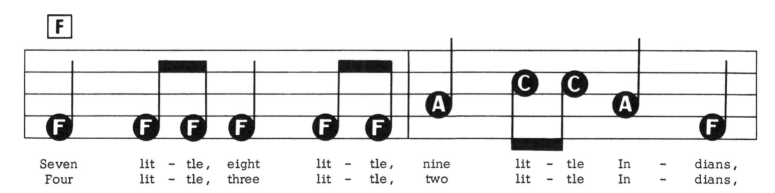

Seven lit - tle, eight lit - tle, nine lit - tle In - dians,
Four lit - tle, three lit - tle, two lit - tle In - dians,

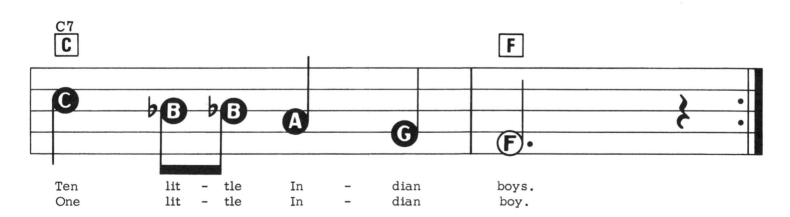

Ten lit - tle In - dian boys.
One lit - tle In - dian boy.

It Ain't Gonna Rain No More

Registration 3

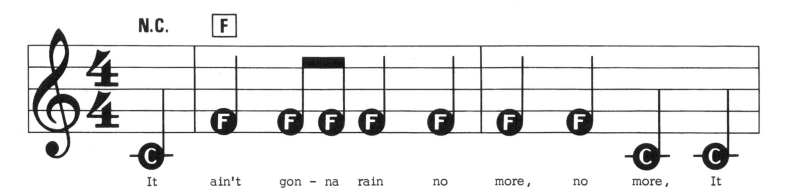

It ain't gon - na rain no more, no more, It

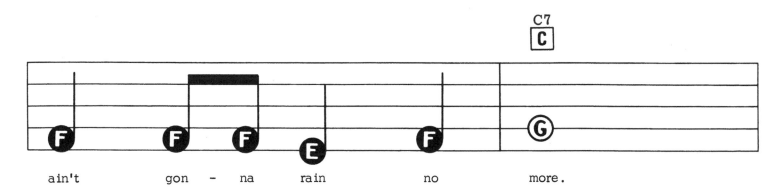

ain't gon - na rain no more.

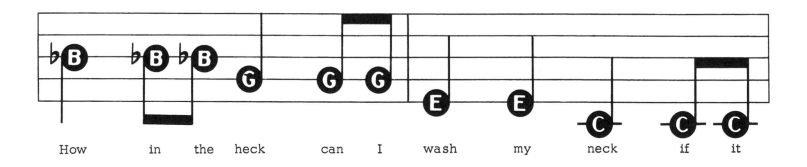

How in the heck can I wash my neck if it

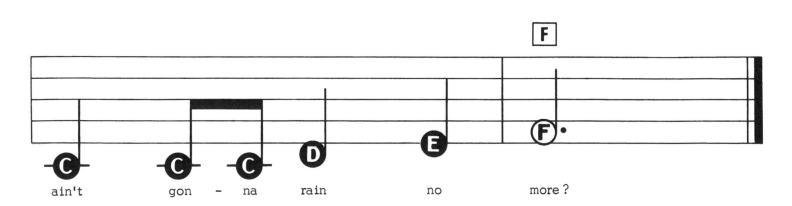

ain't gon - na rain no more?

Chopsticks

This song can be played with BOTH HANDS on the SAME keyboard!

● Play the big notes (with the stems going up) with your RIGHT hand.

● Play the smaller notes (with the stems going down) with your LEFT hand.

It's really fun to play "Chopsticks" this way. But you can play just the big notes with your right hand and the chords with your left hand, too.

Registration 8

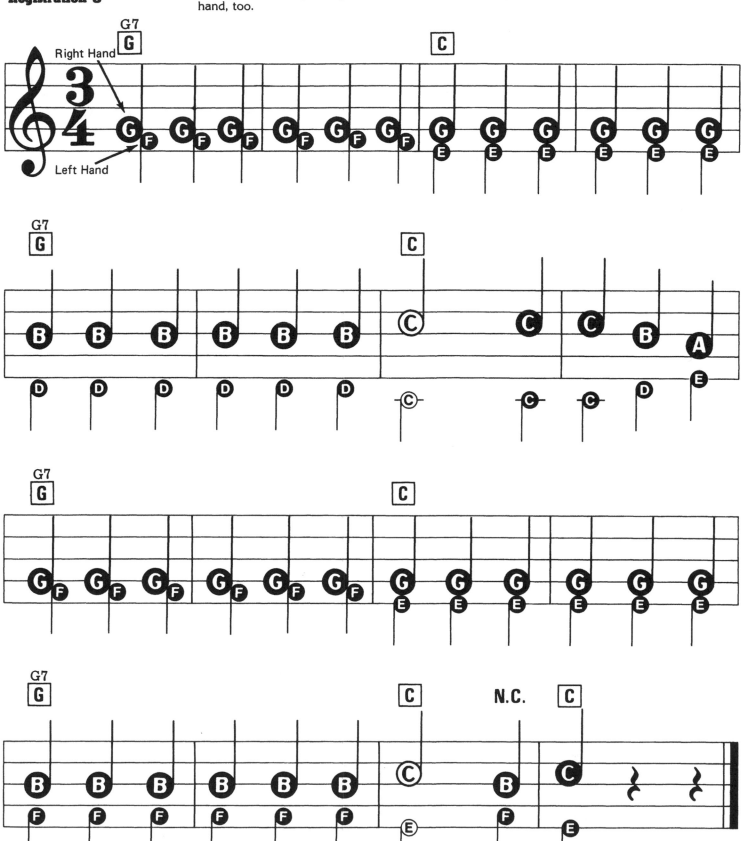

This Old Man

Registration 5

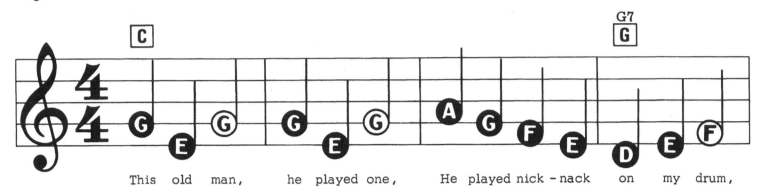

This old man, he played one, He played nick-nack on my drum,

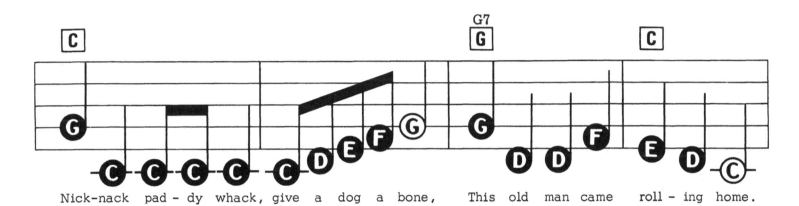

Nick-nack pad-dy whack, give a dog a bone, This old man came roll-ing home.

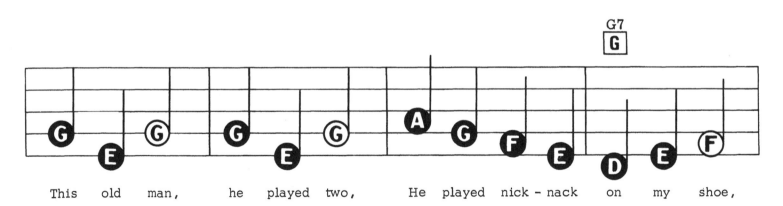

This old man, he played two, He played nick-nack on my shoe,

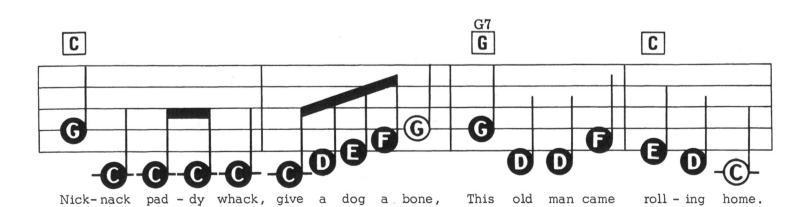

Nick-nack pad-dy whack, give a dog a bone, This old man came roll-ing home.

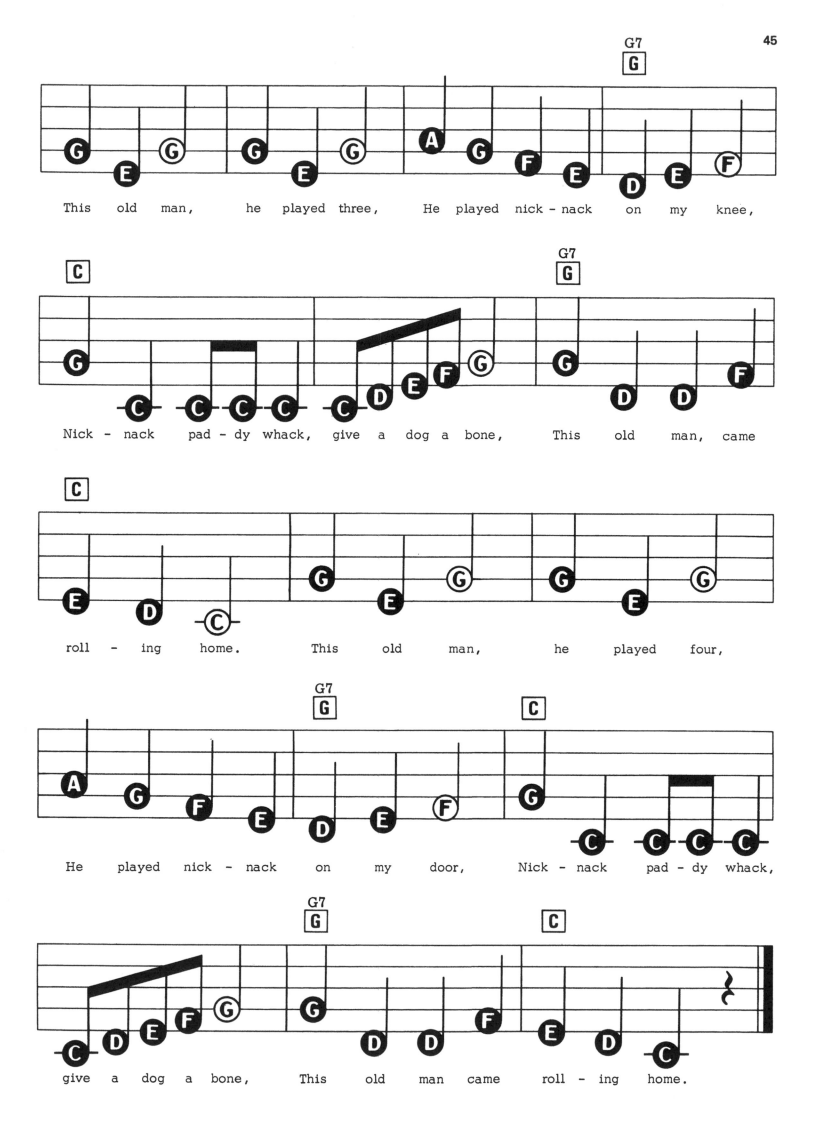

Guitar Chord Chart

To use the E-Z Play TODAY Guitar Chord chart, simply find the **letter name** of the chord at the top of the chart, and the **kind of chord** (Major, Minor, etc.) in the column at the left. Read down and across to find the correct chord. Suggested fingering has been indicated, but feel free to use alternate fingering.

	C	D♭	D	E♭	E	F
MAJOR						
MINOR (m)						
7TH (7)						
MINOR 7TH (m7)						

	F♯	**G**	**A♭**	**A**	**B♭**	**B**
MAJOR						
MINOR (m)						
7TH (7)						
MINOR 7TH (m7)						

Chord Speller Chart
of Standard Chord Positions

For those who play standard chord positions, all chords used in the E-Z Play TODAY music arrangements are shown here in their most commonly used chord positions. Suggested fingering is also indicated but feel free to use alternate fingering.

CHORD FAMILY Abbrev.	MAJOR	MINOR (m)	7TH (7)	MINOR 7TH (m7)
C	5 2 1 G-C-E	5 2 1 G-C-Eb	5 3 2 1 G-Bb-C-E	5 3 2 1 G-Bb-C-Eb
Db	5 2 1 Ab-Db-F	5 2 1 Ab-Db-E	5 3 2 1 Ab-B-Db-F	5 3 2 1 Ab-B-Db-E
D	5 3 1 F#-A-D	5 2 1 A-D-F	5 3 2 1 F#-A-C-D	5 3 2 1 A-C-D-F
Eb	5 3 1 G-Bb-Eb	5 3 1 Gb-Bb-Eb	5 3 2 1 G-Bb-Db-Eb	5 3 2 1 Gb-Bb-Db-Eb
E	5 3 1 G#-B-E	5 3 1 G-B-E	5 3 2 1 G#-B-D-E	5 3 2 1 G-B-D-E
F	4 2 1 A-C-F	4 2 1 Ab-C-F	5 3 2 1 A-C-Eb-F	5 3 2 1 Ab-C-Eb-F
F#	4 2 1 F#-A#-C#	4 2 1 F#-A-C#	5 3 2 1 F#-A#-C#-E	5 3 2 1 F#-A-C#-E
G	5 3 1 G-B-D	5 3 1 G-Bb-D	5 3 2 1 G-B-D-F	5 3 2 1 G-Bb-D-F
Ab	4 2 1 Ab-C-Eb	4 2 1 Ab-B-Eb	5 3 2 1 Ab-C-Eb-Gb	5 3 2 1 Ab-B-Eb-Gb
A	4 2 1 A-C#-E	4 2 1 A-C-E	5 4 2 1 G-A-C#-E	5 4 2 1 G-A-C-E
Bb	4 2 1 Bb-D-F	4 2 1 Bb-Db-F	5 4 2 1 Ab-Bb-D-F	5 4 2 1 Ab-Bb-Db-F
B	5 2 1 F#-B-D#	5 2 1 F#-B-D	5 3 2 1 F#-A-B-D#	5 3 2 1 F#-A-B-D